Keepin...

By Sharon Gordon

Consultants
Nanci Vargus, Ed.D.
Primary Multiage Teacher
Decatur Township Schools, Indianapolis, Indiana

Jayne L. Waddell, R.N., M.A., L.P.C.
School Nurse/Health Educator/Lic. Professional Counselor

Designer: Herman Adler Design
Photo Researcher: Caroline Anderson
The photo on the cover shows a young girl washing her hands.

Library of Congress Cataloging-in-Publication Data

Gordon, Sharon.
  Keeping clean / by Sharon Gordon.
    p. cm. — (Rookie read-about health)
  Includes index.
Summary: Discusses the importance of keeping clean by showering, bathing,
washing hands before eating, and keeping the house clean.
  ISBN 0-516-22572-3 (lib. bdg.)   0-516-26951-8 (pbk.)
  1. Hygiene—Juvenile literature. [1. Hygiene.] I. Title. II. Series.
RA780 .G67 2002

                        2002005483

It is fun to play in the tub!

It is also good for you.

A bath helps keep you clean. It washes away dirt. It gets rid of germs, too.

So grab a towel and some soap. Scrub your hands and face.

Don't forget to wash
behind your ears!

Some people like to shower.
The falling water feels good.

When you are playing a sport, you may start to feel very hot.

Your body tries to stay cool by giving off water through your skin. These drops of water are called sweat.

Sometimes, sweat mixes with the germs on your skin. It makes a bad smell, or odor.

A shower can take away
the sweat and the smell.

Keep clean in between
your baths or showers.
Wash your hands when you
come home from school.

Always wash your hands after you use the bathroom, play outside, or touch animals.

It is also very important to wash your hands before you eat food. You don't want germs to end up in your mouth!

Keep your clothes clean, too.

Sweaty clothes will start to smell. Put those dirty socks in the wash!

Are your teeth clean? You need to brush your teeth at least two times a day.

Brushing your teeth gets rid of the germs in your mouth. These germs can cause bad breath and cavities.

Your home needs to be clean, too. You can help. Start with your own room.

Keep your dishes clean.
Wipe the table after dinner.

Sweep the floor.

Take off your shoes before you come inside.

You don't want to make
the clean floor muddy!

Uh-oh.

Someone forgot to
tell the dog!

Words You Know

bath

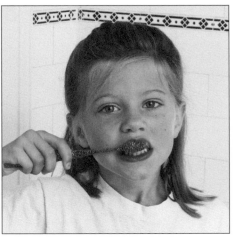

brushing teeth

clean

dirt

muddy

shower

sweat

washing hands

31

Index

About the Author

Sharon Gordon is a writer living in Midland Park, New Jersey. She and her husband have three school-aged children and a spoiled pooch. Together they enjoy visiting the Outer Banks of North Carolina as often as possible.

Photo Credits

Photographs © 2002: Corbis Images/Michael Pole: 3, 30 top left; Peter Arnold Inc./Laura Dwight: 21, 30 top right; Photo Researchers, NY: cover (Ken Cavanagh), 7 (Lawrence Migdale), 23, 30 bottom left (Linda Phillips), 4 (Sylvie Villeger); PhotoEdit: 20 (Myrleen Ferguson Cate), 17, 24 (Tony Freeman), 8, 31 top right (Jeff Greenberg), 25 (Will Hart), 5, 13, 30 bottom right (Michael Newman), 11, 12, 19, 31 bottom left (David Young-Wolff); Rigoberto Quinteros: 6, 14, 18, 26, 27, 29, 31 bottom right, 31 top left.